Building Relationships Through Pastoral Visitation

BRADFORD LYLE

Building Relationships Through Pastoral Visitation

Judson Press ® Valley Forge

BUILDING RELATIONSHIPS THROUGH PASTORAL VISITATION

Copyright © 1984
Judson Press, Valley Forge, PA 19482-0851

All rights reserved. No part of this publication may be reproduced, stored in a retrieval system, or transmitted in any form or by any means, electronic, mechanical, photocopying, recording, or otherwise, without the prior permission of the copyright owner, except for brief quotations included in a review of the book.

The Scripture quotations in this publication are from the Revised Standard Version of the Bible copyrighted 1946, 1952 © 1971, 1973 by the Division of Christian Education of the National Council of the Churches of Christ in the U.S.A., and used by permission.

Library of Congress Cataloging in Publication Data

Lyle, Bradford.
  Building relationships through pastoral visitation.

  Includes bibliographical references.
  1. Visitations (Church work)   I. Title.
BV4320.L95   1984   253.7'6   83-24859
ISBN 0-8170-1006-8

The name JUDSON PRESS is registered as a trademark in the U.S. Patent Office.
Printed in the U.S.A.

Contents

Introduction	7
1 Why Pastoral Visitation Is Important Today	9
2 A Theology and History of Home Visits	15
3 The Role of Listening in Ministry Today	23
4 Kinds of Pastoral Visits	31
5 Visits to Homes	41
6 Training Lay Persons for Visitation	55
7 Conclusion	61
Notes	63

Introduction

Most of us have had an experience of someone coming into our lives who made a difference—a good difference. It may have been an uncle or aunt, a brother or sister, a parent who has been away for some time, a good friend—for some of us, it may have been a minister.

I recall the story of a friend of the family I heard while growing up. During the 1920s this woman with three young children was deserted by her husband. At that time divorce was almost unheard of and there was a certain stigma attached to such circumstances. I remember this fine woman relating how the home visits a pastor made to the family during those most difficult times helped her.

This book has to do with the kind of ministry that pastor offered to a deeply distraught woman many years ago. Most ministers want to provide this kind of ministry of presence for their parishioners. Perhaps the greatest compliment that can be paid to a minister by someone is: "You were there when I really needed you." Times have of course changed. The pace of ministry seems of necessity to be more hectic. Yet there is still something very appropriate in a pastor going to the home of a parishioner to share the faith, offer guidance, better understand a life situation, or simply listen well. The minister is still a "significant other" in the lives of parishioners. What follows is written from a conviction that quality home visits can undergird effective ministry.

The reader will find various dimensions of home visitation—the why, when, and how of this kind of pastoral care—discussed. We will also look at the roots of the home visit in church history, compare different kinds of pastoral visits, underscore the central role of listening in all such visitation, and consider one possible approach for training lay people in visiting within the congregation. The author hopes that what follows will make a contribution toward reclaiming home visits for ministry today.

1
Why Pastoral Visitation Is Important Today

Steve is a young man of twenty-five and a member of our church. He was just told yesterday that his computer sales job had been terminated. Steve spent most of today in the unemployment office waiting in lines, filling out form after form. He and his wife, Jackie, shared supper with us. After the meal he began to talk about computers.

"Someday soon a computer will do our shopping, prepare our meals, and regulate our lives inside and outside the home." His words made me think of a recent article I had seen in the newspaper about the growing use of robots for industrial and domestic work. Are we approaching the time when technology will fully regulate our living? Perhaps, but I, for one, am not looking forward to that time.

The Other Side of Technology

We tend to view technological advances as our friends, and in so many ways machines have made our lives more comfortable and manageable. Because of advances in this area, we have seen people walk on the moon and have witnessed the wonder of the planets close up—exciting! But there is another side to our technological age: it tends to be impersonal. The personal touch is sacrificed for efficiency. There is a story of a college professor who thought she would save time by taping her lectures before classes and leaving the recorder in the classroom to be played back by the students while she did other important things. After several weeks the professor decided to visit the class to see how the idea was working. Opening the door she found on each chair a tape recorder! A moral of this story could be that as we give of ourselves, so we receive.

What is life like for many people today? We are talked at by television and radio, answered on the phone by a machine, do our banking by a combination of mechanized drawer, speaker, and computer. When we meet others and are asked how we are doing, the intent of the question may often be, "How are you doing financially, or who are you socially?" It is in such an atmosphere that we minister today. I believe we are called to minister in the most personal, genuine way we can. We cannot minister to people if we do not know them. Though there are a number of good ways for ministers to come to know parishioners, going to people in pastoral visitation is one of the most effective. The home visit offers a particular opportunity to come to know church members in a setting in which they are comfortable, and for them to come to know the minister better as a pastor and person. Many in the church today seem hungry for such contact with one who will listen, try to understand, advise when asked, and be interested in them as people.

Does Society Shape the Church Too Much?

The church and ministry today can simply reflect the obsession with technical advances and timesaving devices. Certainly these have an important place in our lives today. A computer can help to bring the right minister together with the right church. A phone-answering machine can take important information when the pastor is unavailable. Time management is an important challenge in ministry today where it is so easy to lose control of time. But are we in danger of losing in terms of personal relationship what we gain in efficiency? I can save time making a five-minute phone call to a parishioner compared to an hour-long home visit, not to mention the twenty minutes each way of traveling time. There are occasions in ministry when a phone conversation is all that is needed. But there are also other occasions when the absence of a personal visit means that something special will be lost in the way of face-to-face conversation and the unspoken messages that can be measured only by being there.

I was recently waiting with a woman at the hospital as her husband underwent major surgery. On the wall there was a large sign requesting waiting family members to pick up the phone when it rang so that the doctor could tell them how things went. Apparently many doctors find themselves too busy to come in person to the room and talk to the family member. An advertisement in a newspaper caught my eye. It read: "Remember when doctors used to make house calls? We *still* do!" No, it was not a church ad. An insurance company had placed it. I cut it out and taped it above my desk, for it says something important.

Last night a colleague in ministry phoned. One of his elderly parishioners had suffered a heart attack while visiting her son who lives nearby. Would I take Communion to her in the rehabilitation center? A few days later I stopped by to see the woman. The visit helped me as much as it did her, but she needed more long-term pastoral care than I could offer at that point. I asked if there had been any contact with her church during these past two weeks. No, there had not. I left thinking about priorities in ministry. My colleague has done some good work in his community and church and I do not know all the circumstances. But an elderly woman in a rehabilitation center needs pastoral care from her church, and for various reasons it is not forthcoming, perhaps because it takes an hour and a half of travel time to visit her. Saving time might be important in ministry but it cannot become that important to any of us. Sometimes I wonder: For what are we saving time? If it is to better serve people in the name of Christ, fine. But if it is a masked attempt to avoid contact with people, I question it. We remember the story of Joshua at Gibeon and how God heard his prayer, giving him the time needed for the work before him (Joshua 10:12-14). Might not God be ready to give us the time we need to give the church members the kind of quality pastoral care that is called for? Do we ministers always have to be nervously glancing at our watches or schedule books and follow the premise that "time waits for no one"? I am not saying that pastoral visitation is the most urgent need in ministry today. But I do say that such visitation, including home visitation, is far more important to effective ministry today than many church leaders have either realized or acknowledged in recent years.

Criticism of the Pastoral Visit

The greatest criticism of pastoral visitation, especially the home visit, seems to be that it is a waste of time and car allowance. This week I saw an article on ministry that referred to such visits as "tea" calls. Who wants to waste time sipping a glass of tea with a parishioner? Pastoral calling can be like this. I have experienced visits when I wondered what, if anything, had been accomplished, and feeling my time would have been better spent if the visit had not even been made. But we should be slow to blame the practice of home visitation. Any area of ministry, be it preaching, teaching, counseling, or administration, can be a waste of time if we neither prepare nor are purposeful in our effort. A sermon started at ten o'clock Saturday night will not be worth much the next morning. Neither will a pastoral visit without purpose or forethought. I have learned this the hard way, and now try to keep the question before me: What am I trying to accomplish in this visit? Nurture a pastor/parishioner relationship? Heal a hurt? Seek an opportunity for a person to share more deeply about a concern I suspect is present? Or am I going more for my own benefit this time, in need of an accepting, positive person in the church? All of these are good reasons for a minister to make a visit to the home of a parishioner. There is an elderly woman in our congregation whom I sometimes visit when I feel "down" about things. She has known the loss of her husband after a prolonged and painful illness and she is plagued by a number of health problems herself. But how she can laugh! What a sense of humor and love for living this woman has! I am sure I receive even more from these visits than she does.

Visits Important to People

While there are always some church members who will not welcome a home visit by their ministers, most people welcome such visits. How often do you hear from members of different churches: "Our minister has been here nearly three years now and has never been in our home"? We could answer that this is egotistical thinking. Ministers have more important things to do. Perhaps. But what are people trying to tell us when they say these things? We have traditionally expected people to come to see us at the services of worship, the church school, the programs, our offices. A few years ago a denominational leader remarked at a church conference that Christians are a sent people but the trouble is, they won't go. They keep saying, "Come." There are times when we might more effectively minister to people if we go to where they feel most comfortable. One of those places today is certainly the home. If a person does have a personal concern, that person is more apt to share it in a setting that is familiar to him or her. I think we sometimes underestimate the courage, even a sense of desperation, necessary for many people to make an appointment with the pastor and come to the study to talk. The home visit allows the minister to take the initiative in pastoral care. After several such visits I have found people dropping by the study to pursue a conversation we had begun in the home. What better way to keep in touch with what the people in the church are thinking and concerned about? Such visits can greatly help sermon preparation, programming, and other areas of ministry.

Pastor Needs to Lead the Way

There is a growing practice in churches today to train lay people for home visitation. I believe in this trend. The pastor cannot possibly do all the visiting that needs to be done, especially noncrisis home visiting. Hospital and crisis calling have to take precedence for the pastor. However, lay training for visitation is valuable only if the minister also engages in such visitation and personally considers it important. If the pastor feels that home visiting is a waste of time and is trying to shunt it off to the laity, they will be quick to pick up this feeling, and who wants to spend time and effort on something that is unimportant? The underlying theme of this book is that home visitation by the pastor is important. This sense of importance should be caught and taught to the other members of the church.

2

A Theology and History of Home Visits

A little girl was frightened by a sudden thunderstorm at night. The mother came into the bedroom to comfort her. "Don't worry, honey," her mother said, "you know that God is with you." "I know that, mommy," the girl replied, "but I want somebody with skin on them. . . ." There are times in our lives when we need someone to be present with us—someone "with skin on them." It is in response to this need that pastoral visitation has developed.

Theology of Home Visitation

What theological basis can be given in support of home visits in ministry? Several answers come to mind as we consider this question. How do we believe God has come into our world and lives?

Initiative

We see God taking the initiative with the human race. God did not wait for us to come. God has come to us. The Old Testament is a consistent record of God seeking and finding people in all circumstances of living. Abraham, Isaac, Jacob,

Moses, Samuel, Isaiah, Jeremiah—God found them where they lived with their struggles and questions.

The meaning of incarnation is that the Lord has come to humankind. When the time was full, states the apostle Paul, God sent the Son for our sakes (Galatians 4:4-7). The words of Jesus described God as going out of the way to find especially the wandering and confused (Luke 5:29-32; 15:1-10).

As God has taken the initiative with us, so are pastors empowered to take the initiative with parishioners: to go where they live when parishioners cannot or will not come to us. We do not have to sit passively and watch a marriage or family begin to disintegrate, a church member become alienated, a lonely person endlessly grieve for a departed wife or husband, without doing something to help. We are able to go to people in a way that most other helping professions are not. We need to use this initiative.

Identification

Second, we can see God identifying with humankind in Christ Jesus. The Scriptures remind us that "the Word became flesh and dwelt among us" (John 1:14). The author of Hebrews in the New Testament also points to this close identification:

> For we have not a high priest who is unable to sympathize with our weaknesses, but one who in every respect has been tempted as we are, yet without sin (Hebrews 4:15).

When we go as pastors to homes of parishioners, there should be a point where we identify with the life circumstances of the people we visit. Without this kind of identification it is doubtful whether any effective ministry among the people will ever take place. Most people may not expect the pastor to agree with them all the time, but they do want the pastor to understand the conditions under which they live and work.

Reconciliation

We have been brought close to God and to one another through Christ Jesus. This is a central belief in our Christian faith. The apostle Paul expressed this conviction with the words "All this is from God, who through Christ reconciled us to himself and gave us the ministry of reconciliation" (2 Corinthians 5:18).

There are times when our main reason for going to the home of another parishioner is to encourage reconciliation between us. Some estrangement may be felt during a contact with a church member on Sunday morning or during a weekday meeting. What is the trouble? Can it be overcome? The visit provides an opportunity for reconciliation where possible. God in Christ has come into our territory where we feel at home to bring about reconciliation. So does the pastor go to the home of parishioners where they are less likely to feel threatened.

Seeking such reconciliation may well be the most difficult aspect of ministering through home visitation; our feelings can sometimes get in the way. It is not easy to go to someone who may be causing trouble in our ministry—to go to that person, listen, and respond without letting our anger take over the situation. Many of us tend to put off such visits as long as possible. Yet the opportunity to go to people experiencing inner turmoil is always there, built into pastoral ministry. Facing hostility is never an easy matter, but it is better than the alternatives of denying its reality or letting anger toward certain church members fester within us until it erupts in harmful ways.

Acceptance

Another important belief among Christians is that God comes to us not in judgment but rather in acceptance. The Gospel of John states that ". . . God sent the Son into the world, not to condemn the world, but that the world might be saved through him" (John 3:17).

In his earthly ministry Jesus stressed God's acceptance wherever people turned in sincerity to him. Christ invited those weighed down with care or guilt, commended a woman with a bad reputation for her kind act of anointing with oil, and stressed God's forgiveness for those who wanted to go back to obeying God (Matthew 11:28-30; Luke 7:36-50; 15:11-24).

As pastors we go to homes conveying this same message of acceptance. We go not to criticize or condemn but rather to evidence a concern for these parishioners as people. Sometimes those of us who are deeply involved in the leadership of the church can develop almost unknowingly a harsh attitude toward others—either those outside the church fellowship or perhaps those who have become inactive members. We need periodically to check out such attitudes, doing all we can to rid ourselves of them before home visits are made.

Risk

The last quality we see in considering God's relationship with us is that of risk. By coming to us God became vulnerable to our response. We sense this risk in such well-known words as "God so loved the world that he gave his only Son" (John 3:16); and Jesus' parable of the wicked tenants also conveys this vulnerability. After all else fails, the owner of the vineyard ". . . sent his son to them, saying, 'They will respect my son' " (Matthew 21:37).

When pastors go to homes there is a certain amount of risk involved. Some of us may fear being criticized, being known more as a person, or coming to know parishioners more as people with all the complexities of human relationships. There is also the whole question of being attracted to or repelled by certain personalities. What might happen in such encounters? We never know for certain before going. But we have been given a strong mandate to go to homes as pastors, as God in Christ has come to us—where we live. What follows is a more specific tracing of that mandate from earliest times to the present day.

Old Testament Roots

In the book of Genesis we are told that the Lord paid a spontaneous visit to Adam and Eve, representing all men and women, at the dawn of creation. God asked them: "Where are you?" (Genesis 3:8-9). This is an excellent question on which to build a theology of home visitation. We meet with parishioners in their home settings because we want to know where they are in their living, thinking, and faith. Church members may feel more comfortable in the home setting to ask the pastor, "Where are you? . . . What do you think about this issue, that question?"

We are also told that the angels of the Lord made a home visit on Abraham and Sarah as they dwelt by the oaks of Mamre (Genesis 18:1-15). God's messengers were given refreshments that day by a grateful couple. This sometimes happens in our pastoral visits to homes as well, and sharing food can help conversation and communication. Abraham and Sarah received good news from the visit that hot day; they would have a son at long last. They found this welcome news but hard to believe. As pastors, we hope our visits will be good news for the parishioners as well as for ourselves. But sometimes we, like Sarah, find it hard to believe that good news can come from such visits. Suspicion, cynicism, or preoccupation can hinder the blessing that should be the result of such a meeting in a home. It takes a growing faith and an open mind to bring about a good home visit.

Elisha, the prophet, visited the homes of those he helped, such as the childless woman and the widow with two children (2 Kings 4). Jeremiah was also reported to have paid a visit on more than one occasion to the home of the king (Jeremiah 22:1-2).

Jesus and Home Visits

One of the earliest recorded acts of Jesus' earthly ministry is entering the home of Peter's mother to cure her fever (Mark 1:29). We also recall the incident when Jesus entered the home of Jairus, much to the surprise of cynical onlookers, to raise his daughter from serious illness (Mark 5:35-43). A lasting model for our home visitation is given in the story of Jesus and Zacchaeus. Riding through Jericho, Jesus singled out Zacchaeus, the tax collector, saying, "Zacchaeus, make haste and come down; for I must stay at your house today" (Luke 19:5).

Some of the crowd resented Jesus' going to the home of this sinner. Yet it was through this home visit that Zacchaeus's life was turned around. He began to walk according to God's purpose. Most of the visits we do in our ministries are far different from this dramatic event. But if Christ is present where two or three gather in his name in a home, can we ever predict what the result might be?

Home Visits in History

The early church kept up the practice of home visits as a means of teaching, evangelizing, encouraging, and healing. Ananias, the Damascan Christian, was led to pay a visit to the blinded, confused Saul who was staying on the street called Straight (Acts 9:10-19). How many people today are also staying in temporary housing—rentals, trailers, motel rooms—people often bewildered and unable to see the way they should go, and who are in need of good news? The presence of such need is the reason why evangelistic visits to the homes of those who have come into contact with the church through worship, a wedding, or church school are so important. Who knows? There may be another Saul behind the door, waiting for someone to bring just the right word from God to him. The affluent in our communities also have spiritual needs. Many today have enough material things, status, or influence, but lack the one thing necessary to bring fullness to living—knowing Christ.

Although many changes took place in the church with the coming of the Dark and Middle Ages, the practice of home visits was never entirely abandoned. Theodore of Tarsus, an Archbishop of Canterbury in the seventh century, instructed priests to go to their people for confession when they would not come to the church.[1] In the classic *Canterbury Tales*, Geoffrey Chaucer described in a well-known passage a pastor who faithfully visited parishioners:

> Broad was his parish, with houses far apart,
> Yet come it rain or thunder he would start
> Upon his rounds, in woe or sickness too,
> And reach the farthest, poor or well-to-do,
> Going on foot, his staff within his hand—
> Example that his sheep could understand. . . . [2]

With the coming of the Protestant Reformation in the sixteenth century, church leaders such as Martin Luther were inclined to extend pastoral care to the dwelling places of their people.[3] John Wesley, the great church reformer of eighteenth-century England, also placed a high priority on home visitation.[4] And Ichabod Spencer, a mid-nineteenth-century Presbyterian pastor of New York City after whom the Spencer Memorial Church of Brooklyn is named, developed home visits into an effective ministerial art. According to one of Spencer's present-day commentators, he saw little difference between going to see a parishioner and a parishioner coming to see him.[5] There is an important lesson in that attitude for those of us who practice ministry today.

Throughout this period the home visit was seen almost exclusively as an opportunity for bringing about repentance, teaching, or evangelism. But with the coming of our present century this rigid view began to be tempered with the growing attitude that such visits could be used to extend a gentler form of pastoral care to the home. Washington Gladden, Congregational pastor and author, was called one of the "princes of the pulpit" because of his powerful preaching. But he also placed great emphasis upon pastoral contact with parishioners through home visits. Commenting over seventy years ago upon the problem of brief pastorates, Gladden observed:

> May not the decline of pastoral visitation be in part an explanation of this? The pastor's personal religious life is not brought into contact with the people, and the only bond between them is his preaching; and when the novelty of his voice and manner has passed away, they are not held to him. . . . When he is not faithful to them in private, they feel that he is not earnest in his public performances.[6]

Our present age has not lacked critics of the home visit. With the increasingly hectic pace of living, some prominent church leaders have questioned such a practice as having little or no lasting value. Yet in more recent times pastoral visitation to homes has had an equal number of impressive champions. Wayne Oates, an influential voice in the area of pastoral care for over three decades, has consistently pointed to home visits as an effective instrument for ministry.[7] Paul Pruyser, a clinical psychologist, has also been a strong advocate of such visitation in the pastorate.[8] These are but two of a growing number of advocates for home visits in the area of pastoral care today.

Attitudes Among Contemporary Ministers

What of pastors today? Is there a positive attitude toward the home visit? I recently did a professional research project on this subject and received some interesting responses. Of twenty-four ministers from varying denominations and backgrounds questioned, the majority valued the importance of home visitation—especially for nurturing relationships with parishioners. Quality rather than quantity of visits was seen to be of greatest importance, and afternoons or evenings were the most popular times of day for such calling. The length of these visits averaged between one-half to two hours, depending on circumstances. Most of these pastors indicated that they tried to be intentional when making such personal calls to homes. They visited with a certain purpose in mind. Such visits were usually made after a need had been perceived. The approaches most often used among these pastors in home visits were to listen actively, show concern, offer suggestions or information and resources, and share the faith where there was opportunity to do so.

Despite criticism in recent years it seems that home visiting has never really been very far from the ministry of the conscientious pastor. In carrying out such pastoral care to homes, we are part of a tradition that stretches back to the early church and beyond, to the very beginnings of God's people.

3

The Role of Listening in Ministry Today

Nothing is so important yet so neglected in our living as good listening. There is a story of three friends who went into town on a bus. The first friend remarked, "Isn't it windy?" The second answered, "No . . . I think it's Thursday"; to which the third friend replied, "So am I . . . let's get something to drink." Advertisements tell us that companies are losing millions of dollars each year because of poor listening, and educators fear the consequences in the classroom. The attitude of our society is often not very helpful at this point. Being a good listener is usually seen as secondary to being a person of action. Whoever heard of a popular movie or television series in which the hero or heroine was a good listener? Yet as we look toward Jesus, we see one who not only acted in responsible ways but also listened carefully to what others were saying. We see this quality of good listening throughout his ministry—with the woman at the well, the rich young man, and even with his enemies (John 4:7-26; Mark 10:17-22; Matthew 22:15-33). Always, Jesus listened for the human motives and meanings behind the words.

Like anyone else, ministers can fall into poor listening habits.

Listening is hard work. Sometimes it is far easier for us to tune out conversation that we feel does not concern us or that we find uninteresting. The nature of ministry also influences us toward spreading ourselves too thinly in our work. We can become so preoccupied with everything needing to be done that we do not hear what another person is saying. These are some of the particular problems of good listening in ministry. Are there any answers?

Hindrances to Good Listening

As mentioned earlier, I conducted a professional project in the church involving extensive home visitation. One reason for my increasing interest in pastoral home visits was based on the feeling that some concerns of parishioners were not being heard. I thought the home setting might provide a favorable setting to improve listening skills. One question in my research asked what specific attitudes or behavior on the pastor's part might inhibit parishioners from talking about personal concerns during a visit. Some of the responses were: talking too much, giving the impression of being rushed, nervousness, irritability, too much attention to things rather than people, and defensiveness. Taken together, these kinds of behavior define the major reasons for less than effective listening in ministry.

One home visit made during this time to a retired couple in our congregation was on a day when I felt tired and rushed. On the parishioner's evaluation form the wife noted that I had seemed preoccupied during the conversation. Some of the obstacles to good listening had stood in the way. I try to remember this lesson in pastoral visiting: If you are feeling too rushed and tired, do not visit if you can possibly delay it. There are, of course, circumstances in ministry when we cannot avoid visiting with parishioners when we are tired. This is especially true in times of personal crisis for a church member or family. In such situations we especially need to rely on God's strength to carry us through.

Unspoken Messages

After every visit made during my professional project I filled out a self-evaluation form about the conversation in the home. Among the questions was one that asked if I had perceived any unspoken messages from the people. Had I been listening between the lines to what had been said, or not said?

The area of what we now term "body language" was relevant at this point and helped in evaluating these visits. Following my first call on a church couple I observed that they were sitting stiffly in their chairs. By the second visit this stiffness had disappeared. The husband even had his arm around his wife during part of our time together. These changes in posture indicated to me that they were no longer threatened by my presence and did not feel defensive.

On visiting the home of another couple, physical behavior conveyed signs of family tension and a reluctance to deal with it. Following my arrival the husband kept watching television for a time as if to say, "I'm really not looking forward to getting into some of our concerns as a family." The wife came in later, sat with her arms folded during our meeting and said almost nothing. During the second visit the wife was absent altogether. I have a good relationship with both of these people. They are supportive of me and continue to be so, but they were not ready at that particular time to share their personal concerns with anyone. Timing, as with all areas of ministry, is important in home visits.

Such observations on body language and behavior can augment our listening during a pastoral visit. Ear and eye work together with the words we choose in conversation. What might have happened if I had remarked to the quiet woman with her arms folded: "You don't seem to be saying much, is there anything wrong?" Or, if a pastor is talking with someone whose words seem filled with anxiety, it might be helpful to say, "You are really upset about this" or, "Is there some other side of this matter that is troubling you?" We need to use discretion here. Sometimes it is helpful to risk such a comment and at other times not. Putting our observation into words might either open up a deeper dimension to our pastoral conversation or end it. We have to use our own judgment and, most of all, rely upon the guidance of the Spirit.

There are many perceptions that can help us to be more effective in our pastoral calling. If you are visiting a couple or family, who does most of the talking? Do they seem tense or at ease with each other? Are they sitting close together or far apart?

Do pets seem to have the run of the house? Does the television or radio remain on during your visit? All of these observations can help us in more fully understanding the lives and concerns of our parishioners.

How Do We Listen Better?

How do we become better listeners in ministry? It takes effort to listen well. In so doing, we momentarily block out our own thoughts and concerns while focusing upon the other person. Recently a popular comedy show depicted a woman sitting in a restaurant. No one listened to or even noticed her. The waiters, other customers, even the woman's companion—all acted as if she were not there. This was intended to be funny, but it was also very sad and too true in the experiences of many people. Everyone fears not being recognized or listened to and most church members seem to fear not being noticed by other members or by their minister. Even casual attenders live in the hope that the pastor will listen to them, not because the pastor is paid by the hour to do so, but rather because they hope the pastor believes they are important. One of the questions parishioners were asked to answer on the evaluation forms following visits was, "Did you feel the pastor was listening?" Indications of good listening were cited, such as: looking at them while talking, not interrupting, responding to questions asked, referring to what has been said, making appropriate comments, keeping the conversation moving, and appearing interested in what is being said. These responses can serve as a help toward becoming better listeners in pastoral work. There is much truth in the statement that there is no such thing as an uninteresting person or conversation, only disinterested listeners.

But perhaps the most important clue to becoming better listeners is to keep before us the importance of what people have to say. No matter who a person is, her or his story is important and worth the time to listen. The central message of our gospel is that people matter so much to God that God gave the Son for them (John 3:16). Are we able to try to enter into another's situation through careful listening—to stand in that person's shoes while at the same time withholding our judgment? This is not an easy task, especially for those of us who have been taught to place value judgments consistently on ourselves and others. It is so easy, even in the pastoral ministry, to spend most of our time with those whom we like while if possible avoiding those we dislike—the hostile, resentful, or negative people of the church. To try standing in their shoes for a time, to open ourselves to listen to them, is the real challenge.

Not long ago I visited an elderly woman in our congregation. She had seemed to have led a life of relative ease and now lived in a beautiful condominium. When I talked with this woman with her coiffured hair and stylish clothes, I discovered that she had been born and raised in a small coal town of northeastern Pennsylvania. Her family consisted of eight children, and the father spent most of his adult life in the mines to support them. He, along with her eldest brother, had died at an early age of black lung disease. After marrying, she and her husband left that area and were able to prosper economically, but several years ago she suddenly lost him to a fatal illness. During the past two years this woman has been coping with a cancer that the doctors hope to control. A life of relative ease? Far from it! I share this story to illustrate how much we often do not know about our parishioners until we take the time to go to their homes and listen. Her story has given me an understanding and appreciation that I did not really have before. Should I be called to minister to her during another life crisis, I can now do so more effectively.

Older adults are not the only people who wait for someone to listen to their story. A youth runs away from home, leaving a note for his parents. The note says that he is going in search of somebody who has the time to listen to him because no one at home seems to have the interest. And what about children? Are they in need of someone who will listen with undivided attention? Certainly. Whatever our age or phase of living, we are all looking for persons who will listen to us. It is unfortunate that for so many it is so difficult to find good listeners.

Can Listening Change Anything?

What difference can good listening make? Might it change the direction of human lives? This was a question the late Allen Dulles kept asking himself. In 1917 Dulles was serving on the staff of the American Embassy in Berne, Switzerland. Late one afternoon in April, Dulles's phone rang. A heavily-accented man introducing himself as Vladimir Ilyich Lenin urgently asked to speak to someone at the embassy later in the day. But most of the senior staff had already left and Dulles had an important date with a young woman in an hour. He told Lenin to come to the embassy when it opened at ten the next morning. Lenin protested but Dulles remained firm and hung up the phone.

Lenin did not come to the embassy the next morning, or ever. He journeyed back to Russia by train and took total control of the fledgling Communist revolution. Dulles often reflected later in his career the possible difference it might have made to millions of people had he taken the time to listen to a Russian exile that April afternoon of 1917.[1]

The story of Zacchaeus and Jesus mentioned earlier is a familiar one in the church. Zacchaeus was a person who was changed by meeting and receiving Jesus as a guest. We know that Jesus' words to Zacchaeus had a great effect. But certainly there must also have been some careful listening on the part of Jesus as Zacchaeus shared his story. Listening can make a vital difference in the course of a human life.

In Taylor Caldwell's novel *The Listener*, a man builds a chapel. People can come day or night to have a mysterious somebody listen to them. Most of these individuals at first suspect that "the listener" is a person from one of the helping professions working on a rotating shift with associates. But once in the chapel, these people find great release in just having someone listen. There seems to be a compassionate and understanding presence with them. Alongside the blue curtain that hides the listener is a button that will reveal who this mysterious someone is. As the curtain opens, each individual in his or her own way is strangely encouraged. They all immediately understand why this one would know what they are going through, whether the problem be injustice, impending death, loss of a loved one, pain, or fear. They begin to take on a new strength found in the one who listens. As the story concludes we discover that a lifelike replica of Jesus on the cross is the one behind the curtain—the one who listens. Each person leaves the chapel remembering that he or she does not have to face problems alone.[2]

We look around the congregation on Sunday morning and see people of all ages and circumstances: children with all their new experiences and questions; young people undergoing emotional and physical changes so rapidly that even they cannot keep up with themselves; single adults and young married couples with their particular pressures and pace of living; the middle-aged, at the peak of their powers; and the older adults, experiencing leisure time but also coping with various kinds of loss. Yet one need we all have in common is a ministry of good listening.

4

Kinds of Pastoral Visits

Different circumstances in the lives of people call for different kinds of pastoral visits. This book is mainly about noncrisis visits—pastors making calls at parishioners' homes when there is no clear-cut emergency. To understand better the nature and potential of such visits we need to place them in perspective with other kinds of pastoral calling. How does a routine home visit compare with a crisis visit, hospital call, visit to a prison, mental hospital, or nursing home? We now turn to this question.

Hospital Visits

When parishioners are hospitalized they are usually in pain, feeling anxiety, and in need of personal support. Hospital visits are therefore necessary for pastors and should be given priority in pastoral visitation. Most pastors seem to be aware of this. So much excellent material has been written on hospital ministry that I will make only a few comments.

Hospitals are a kind of "neutral zone" for pastor and parishioner. Contact takes place neither at church nor in the home. The hospital is, in fact, the domain of medicine and the medical profession—doctors, technicians, nurses, life-support machines, intravenous tubes, charts, and blinking monitors. Many ministers seem to feel quite at home in this environment. I confess I never completely have. Pastors are guests in a hospital, allowed to see patients because of the help they represent.

It is important to remember that hospitals can be scary places for persons of all ages—children in pain who have never been away from parents, the elderly who may fear they will never come out alive, married people separated by illness. No one looks forward to being hospitalized. This is why it is so important for ministers to visit people there.

What is the best way to make such a visit? You might find as many answers as there are pastors. Here are some personal observations:

1. If the hospital allows it, I try to make the visit during a time when there are no visiting hours. After all, my main concern is the patient. Going during visiting hours may mean getting there when two or three friends or relatives are also present. Neither the patient nor I may be able to say what needs to be said. One exception to this rule is when I also want to see the immediate family along with the person hospitalized. Such a time can usually be arranged beforehand.

2. Patients understandably appreciate a pastoral visit before surgery, which can be an anxious time for an individual. I always try to get to see someone in the hospital on the day before surgery is scheduled. After talking, I leave a booklet of prayers and Scriptures and have a prayer with the patient.

If surgery the next day is of a serious nature, I follow the practice of many pastors and make myself available to the family at the hospital during the time of the operation.

3. I try to keep the visit brief, usually no longer than ten or fifteen minutes. Our task as pastors is to bring comfort and strength to those who are anxious and in pain. There will be others visiting, and medical staff will be in and out to do their work. We need to be sensitive not to overstay the visit.

4. Should a sleeping patient be awakened? I think it depends. Following surgery the patient may need sleep more than she or he needs to see the pastor at that point. If it appears the patient is napping, I sometimes call the person's name softly or ask the roommate, if there is one, how long the person has been asleep,

and use my discretion about waking the patient.

5. If something bothers me about the lack of proper attention for the patient and the patient has been unable to tell the staff, I find it helpful to stop at the nurse's desk on the way out to talk with someone. It never hurts to let the staff know that outsiders care about those in the hospital.

Visits to Nursing Homes

There has been significant improvement in many of these institutions over the last thirty years. With the ever-increasing number of individuals who need such care, however, many nursing homes are overcrowded. In such conditions adequate care for residents can diminish. It is therefore very important that churches take an interest in these care facilities.

One of the improvements over the years in these institutions has been the increasing use of community volunteers to visit nursing homes, providing services to residents such as crafts, games, entertainment, or simply a one-to-one relationship. When such contact with church and community people is maintained, institutional conditions are almost certain to improve.

Most pastors have at various times visited nursing homes when a parishioner is in residence or to lead a service of worship. One factor which may lead some ministers to make few, if any, visits to these institutions might be a fear about the aging process which is so evident there. We need to overcome this fear. The need of ministry in such places is too great to avoid.

As a rule, visiting nursing home residents can be more flexible than visiting in any other setting for pastoral care. Aside from therapy sessions or mealtimes, persons in nursing homes have relatively open schedules. Even if the visit is made during some activity time, I have yet to meet a volunteer or staff person who minded if I took a resident back to a room or lounge area for a visit.

What can we expect in visiting the elderly in nursing homes? Frequently the person has a brief attention span, especially as intellectual faculties begin to fail. But this process varies greatly with individuals. Some ninety-year-olds are still mentally alert and evidence good memories. If senility is present to any great degree, it has been my experience that trying to share Communion is futile because the meaning of the bread and cup has been forgotten. The ministry of presence—just being there in the name of Christ—takes on great significance under such circumstances.

We should also remember that not all residents of nursing homes are elderly people. There are usually a few younger persons living in the facility—victims of various illnesses or accidents that have left them disabled. Conversations with these individuals might tend to be different in content and approach from talks with the elderly. On one occasion I brought some members of our church's senior youth fellowship to participate in an afternoon worship service at a local convalescent center. A rehabilitation facility was adjacent to the home, and some younger individuals facing illness or serious injury were also present. Following worship we visited with the young patients who had come to the service. This experience had an effect on some of the church youth. Most of them had never been able to talk with younger people in such circumstances. They want to go again! But whatever the age of nursing home residents, pastors in a special way represent God's caring when we take the time to visit them.

Visits to Mental Institutions[1]

In a similar way pastors may put off visits to residents in mental hospitals because such an illness can trigger feelings of anxiety or guilt. Another difficulty is that we are accustomed to talking with persons who are rational. We may not always agree with their attitudes or behavior but we can usually carry on a conversation that makes sense. This is frequently not the case with those in a mental hospital setting. Words and behavior in many cases will not make sense to us. This can be threatening to the person visiting, whether pastor or lay person. Yet chaplains in such institutions seem convinced that visits from persons in the community can be beneficial to patients. How, then, should the leadership of the church proceed in such a ministry?

While normal conversation may not always be possible in the setting of a mental hospital, a ministry of presence—being there for a certain length of time with the patient—can often do much good. I recall a seminary professor relating how as a young pastor he had once made weekly visits to a deeply depressed woman in a mental hospital. After a while he could detect a slight sign of recognition in the patient's eyes. One week he could not make the visit. The next time he went to the hospital the woman had regressed to a state of complete withdrawal. Our visits to such persons do make a difference even when results are not immediately apparent. A problem in all pastoral visitation, especially in visits such as we are now discussing, is that the results are not always immediately recognizable or measurable. In a society that demands accomplishment, this kind of ministry seems difficult to justify. But in the simple approach of attempting to be there with another person, healing often begins to take place.

It is important to phone first before making such visits. Because of the therapy and special activities in such institutions, the schedule is often rigid. It is also helpful to have an introductory grasp of the nature of mental illness. This can be acquired by reading, conversations with chaplains or doctors, or some kind of orientation session before making a visit to a mental hospital.

Visits to Prisons

Feelings of fear or guilt can also be generated in visiting jails or prisons. Yet we have a clear mandate from Christ to undertake such visitation (Matthew 25:36). Jails and prisons are institutions that by nature limit outside contacts, for security as well as punitive reasons. Access to prisoners varies greatly according to the particular prison. This can sometimes be predetermined by the terms "maximum" or "minimum" security. But even these terms are not always accurate guidelines. What matters seems to be the overall philosophy of the prison. Security is always the primary concern of those in charge.

I have made visits to a parishioner in a large state prison. As long as I went during certain set hours, I found no problem in making the visit. I have also had the experience of trying to visit another parishioner in a county jail where the visiting hours kept changing, little consideration was given to local clergy, and the attitude toward outsiders was overly suspicious. A fortress mentality can develop too easily in such places, and this doesn't encourage pastors to make visits. But perhaps these are the very facilities that are most in need of pastoral perseverance.

Many prisons, and even some small jails, have part- or full-time chaplains who are partially or wholly supported by the institution. Some prisons prefer to have these persons deal with all pastoral needs. Many of these chaplains do manage to minister with effectiveness to the needs of prisoners under difficult circumstances. Some inmates, however, see such chaplains as part of the system that is punishing them and therefore mistrust institutional clergy. In such cases a pastor visiting from the outside may be able to help a particular inmate very effectively.

When should pastors make visits to a jail or prison? Certainly a visit is appropriate when a parishioner, relative of a church family, or acquaintance with no religious affiliation is incarcerated. Another circumstance would be if the penal institution had no chaplain assigned to it. A third instance might be if a jail or prison had a particularly bad reputation for poor conditions. A pastoral visit in this case could be helpful in making the facility staff aware that responsible leaders of the community care about life behind the walls and inside the bars.

For reasons of security it is important that ministers let the prison know beforehand when they plan to visit. Most facilities have a definite procedure for visiting inmates and are strict about enforcing it. In preparation for a visit it would be helpful to learn as much as possible about what life is like on the inside of the institution. As in the case of visiting mental hospitals, this can be done through reading, talking with knowledgeable persons, or attending some kind of orientation or discussion session on prison life.

It is also necessary to know the rules of certain institutions which we visit and to abide by those rules. We are being trusted to follow the procedure laid down by those in authority. The prison system, of course, needs much reform, and the church needs to work for this. In the meantime, pastors are called to bring ministry to needy persons in admittedly imperfect and too often unjust institutions.

Once inside the prison and talking to an inmate, how should we proceed? Certainly listening—the ministry of presence—is important here. We can try to come to the prisoner as persons of warmth and honesty. Care should be taken to avoid the attitude that sees the prisoner as another potential convert, to be turned dramatically away from a degenerate life. We can go in humility, seeking to witness to the love and presence of Christ but leaving conversion in his hands where it surely belongs.

Most prisons or jails also allow a certain period of time for talking with an inmate, after which visitors are requested to leave. We need to take this time frame into account when visits to inmates are made, for it determines what our approach to the conversation will be.

Today there are opportunities for lay people to participate in prison ministry as at no other time before. Volunteer groups, varying in emphasis from Bible study sessions to teaching courses and skills, have begun in various communities where prisons are located.

In his story *Return to the World*, ex-convict Lawrence Baulch tells of being initially influenced in prison by a Christian Science lay person who visited the institution weekly. In time, with the help of a chaplain, Baulch matured in his faith beyond this teaching but the incident underscores the critical importance of trained persons to visit inmates.[2] Marie Buckley has related in her writing the shameful example of a young man who spent nine months in a prison without having one person visit him from the outside.[3] The church does have a ministry to prisons and visitation is the basis of that ministry.

Home Visits

I would distinguish three kinds of home visits in ministry today—the evangelistic visit, the crisis visit, and the routine visit.

Evangelistic Visit

An evangelistic visit is one that is made upon people who are not church members—those who have recently attended worship or church school, or persons married in the sanctuary. Such a visit gives the pastor and church members opportunity to know community people better, share their faith when appropriate, and thereby seek a commitment or recommitment to Christ, the local congregation, or both. Many excellent books and articles have been written about this kind of home visitation. I refer the reader to them, while sharing one simple approach used by the congregation I presently serve. On most Sunday evenings a team of lay people and the pastor make visits on those who have had recent contact with our congregation. These community people have been phoned earlier in the day or week and know of our coming. Though some say, "No, thank you," most are receptive to a visit once they understand its purpose. We visit in teams of two, bringing relevant information and material about the church with us. We have conversation with the people and respond to any questions they may have about the church or, if newcomers, about the community. These visits are usually closed with prayer. Most of the time the people offer some kind of refreshment, and conversation continues around the table. These meetings last about one hour.

It has been our experience that such visits to homes are very important. Many of these people have eventually joined our congregation. Such contact seems to give people the message that we think they are important enough to take the time and make the effort to visit them. A letter or phone call does not fill the void if such personal contact from the pastor and lay people is not also forthcoming.

Crisis Visit

The crisis home visit is known to every pastor. The phone rings just as the pastor is sitting down to supper. It is Mrs. Johnson. The police are looking for Fred, her oldest boy. The house is in an uproar, with everybody blaming everyone else. There is a long history of family tensions here and mentally the pastor reviews the background while speaking with the caller. "Can you come over soon?" A call to the chairperson of the committee scheduled to meet tonight warns of delay and the pastor prepares for a visit with the Johnson family in order to help them in this time of crisis.

Or, it is two A.M. The phone rings. It is Mrs. White, an elderly member of the congregation. Her husband has been in the hospital this past week following a heart attack. His condition seemed to be improving but the hospital has just called: Mr. White died twenty minutes ago. The pastor immediately offers to go over to the White home for a while, to be present in this time of crisis.

The list could go on and on. These are the kinds of situations that arise very suddenly in a church and a pastor needs to be ready to deal with them. Such home visits are nearly always initiated by the parishioner in a time of personal turmoil or grief.

In this way they differ from regular home visits that are usually set up by the pastor.

Are there any guidelines for crisis home visits? The first question that we need to answer is: Is this really a crisis? This is not easy to answer when we consider the lives of people. Certainly there is no formula that will give us the right guidance every time. It requires an ever-growing knowledge of our congregation, increasing confidence in our judgment and most importantly the guidance of the Spirit. If there is a genuine crisis, the pastor wants to be with that person or family. But some people, due to their own personal problems, have developed demanding tendencies. They want the pastor to drop everything else and rush to them whether the crisis is real or not. I remember a person in the first church I served suffering from the disease of alcoholism. He would frequently phone in the early morning hours and want me to come right over for a talk. The next morning he would not even remember the phone call, my visit, or the rambling one-sided conversation that made little or no sense. I, on the other hand, tried to make it through the day red-eyed, tired, and angry in a way I could not quite define. Were it not for a reformed alcoholic in our church who gave me some much-needed education on this subject, I would still be on that "merry-go-round" of late night visits on demand. I learned that it was far more helpful to wait until the next day, or whenever such a person is sober, to make a personal visit. This is when a pastor can do some good.

Other examples come to mind such as the person in the congregation who phones on your day off and wonders if you could come over right now to talk, even though you have made five other such visits on demand this year and every time you go this person seems to be in good health. The list could go on. Pastors have to determine in their own minds and hearts: Is it really an emergency? Can it wait until morning? Sometimes these questions are not easy to answer. But as much as we are inclined to say "yes" when a request is made of us, we also on occasion need to learn to say "no."

Routine Visit

This kind of visit is the focus of our discussion in this book. Such a visit can help to develop a stronger relationship between pastor and parishioner, begin to address tension in a family or marriage, or simply be helpful by providing a nonthreatening atmosphere in which various hopes or concerns are shared. When such visits are made upon those physically unable to attend church, Communion may be a central part of the time together.

What subjects may be discussed in the course of conversation? Topics such as death and dying, guilt, occupation and retirement, world and national issues, and loneliness have been some of the topics frequently discussed in home visits I have made. I almost never found a lack of content for conversation on such visits. They helped me as a pastor in a number of ways, and I believe they also ministered to the parishioners. More details on the purpose, approach, and results of routine home visits are found in the following chapter.

5

Visits to Homes

On the verge of retirement and looking back over forty-two years of ministry, W. McFerrin Stowe, a Methodist bishop, offers the following insight to those still in the pastorate:

> A visit to a home can open doors for ministry that one never dreamed [were] so badly needed. Remember, everyone is fighting a hard battle, and a loving, caring pastor can help someone win a battle that otherwise would be lost.
> I think that is what this job is all about. Jesus seemed to have the same idea. He visited a lot.[1]

But do other ministers of various denominations agree?

In my survey, pastors were asked to list some of the reasons why they did home visitation. Responses included the following: help rendered to the family, getting to know church people better, affirmation and appreciation from parishioners, reconciliation, stability for the church, and help with preaching.

As to some of the reasons for not engaging in home visits more often, pastors cited the following factors: too few visible results, difficulty finding people at home, distance, open office policy (members encouraged to drop in or make appointments), use of the telephone, and the difficulty of breaking away from some people when a visit is made. Most of us are familiar with all these reasons. Yet when we can make the needs of the people our priority in ministry rather than trying to fit people into various programs, many of these obstacles begin to diminish. We will now look in more detail at these questions concerning home visits in ministry.

Why a Home Visit?

Why should ministers make home visits that are not of a crisis nature? I can only share my experience. At times I have made noncrisis home visits because of some evident tension in the lives of parishioners. People tend to feel more at ease in their own homes and usually welcome such a time with the pastor. Or perhaps I have sensed a distance growing between myself and certain people in the church. A visit to the home might provide an opportunity to resolve the trouble. Even if it doesn't, at least I have shown a concern for them. Good communication between ministers and lay people is very important in our day. When pastor-parish problems develop, it is often in this area of communications. Or it may be that I feel the need to discuss some aspect of the church with a certain member. If circumstances prevent some other people from coming to the church, I feel the need to go to them with some kind of consistency.

Home visits have revealed some needs of parishioners which can be met through pastoral care in home visitation. I have found the most frequently discussed concerns of church members on home visits to be the following.

Mission and Work of the Church

Many persons have far more questions about the local congregation and wider church, including theological questions, than we may suspect. Concerns as to why good people suffer or how long the world can continue to exist in such a crisis condition are frequently expressed during home visits. Church groups, regardless of how small, can inhibit individuals from asking questions that are of real concern to them. We easily forget that some church members are like the paralytic by the pool of Bethzatha who was kept back by others every time he tried to get into the water (John 5:1-9). A few individuals can dominate a discussion, giving the quieter ones little or no opportunity to enter in with their thoughts. The home visit gives people an opportunity to ask questions about the church, Scriptures, or theology that they had not felt able to voice in church settings.

As we have seen, ministers used home visits for instruction in the faith in the earlier days of the church. Classes and groups have gradually taken over this educative function. But should we completely forget this aspect of home visitation used so effectively by church leaders of an earlier day? This is an important question as we consider home visitation in our time.

Need for Prayer

Many church members today are concerned about prayer and its effect in their lives. They may not attend the midweek prayer service or be willing to pray in public, but the act of prayer is important to them—more than we might initially assume.

In my home visits I have found that most people want prayer at the close of the visit. This is more than perfunctory. What we do in such a prayer is lift all the concerns and hopes of our conversation before God and ask that God work in all of them. Once again the roots of prayer together in homes go back to earliest times. Without this effort to be in touch with the Holy Spirit, our efforts in visitation become dry and meaningless. We need also to reclaim this dimension of home calling.

Need for Relating to the Pastor

Another frequent need I have noticed among parishioners in home visits is to know the pastor more as a person. I realize the importance of the pastor's role and the certain aspect of "set-apartness" that is necessary to minister in a congregation. But if pastors become too locked into this role, they can grow stilted or narrow in their functioning. There are times when it is a good and healthy thing to let our humanity show through. Persons can relate only to someone who is also a person to them. A passage from the New Testament letter to the Hebrews comes to mind: ". . . In the days of his flesh, Jesus offered up prayers and supplications, with loud cries and tears . . ."(Hebrews 5:7).

People have to know Jesus as a person before they know him as Savior. So, too, parishioners need to know pastors as people who care for them. The home setting is conducive to enriching such a relationship between pastors and church members.

Need to Share Thoughts and Feelings

It seems to me that most people today are not really encouraged to share their sincere thoughts, feelings, and questions. This holds true even in many church gatherings. A strange silence often seems to pervade the arena of local, national, and world issues in the church. Many people seem to fear self-disclosure in larger groups. The home visit offers an opportunity for pastors and church members to talk openly. Although this does not always happen in home visits, the home setting is conducive to meeting more as friends. At least we have the lasting example of One who described his disciples with this word, with all its implied risk (John 15:15).

Family Concerns

Sooner or later in home visitation, family concerns surface. There are many pressures today on the family. Husbands and wives can find it difficult to communicate. The worlds of adults and children often seem far apart and the generations have trouble relating to one another. There is also the question of authority in a family. How are decisions made? Is compromise or decree the means of determining family direction? It has been observed that when spiritual breakdown takes place in a society, moral breakdown soon follows. We see evidence of such a breakdown but also some signs that many families are coming to realize the deep need for God in their lives together.

The home setting once again offers an appropriate environment for pastor and parishioner to discuss family concerns. The depth of this sharing will depend on the readiness of parishioners to discuss the issues and the trust in which the pastor is held. We can be sure that there are a number of such concerns beneath the surface of our conversations with people.

These topics, then—church, prayer, pastor as person, sharing of thoughts, family concerns—have been the most frequent subjects of my pastoral conversations in homes. They contribute toward an even stronger case for home visits in ministry today.

Bad Reasons for a Visit

Is there such a thing as a bad reason for a noncrisis home visit? Stopping to see members simply because you happen to be in the area is not the best of reasons, although I have done this more than once. It seems to me that all visitation should be done with a purpose in mind. You go because you sense a specific need for pastoral care or are concerned about your relationship with these people. You might visit out of a concern related to the church, or because the member is unable to come to see you. But visiting for no other reason than being in the area does not seem to be a very good foundation for an effective visit.

What about area, or neighborhood visiting—that is, making visits at a certain time in a specific part of the town or county? This is fine when it can be arranged and priority given to the needs of members. It is my belief that the quality of a pastoral visit should always take precedence over the quantity. Suppose you have set aside a certain afternoon for visiting. You could, allowing no more than thirty minutes for each visit, make as many as five or six visits before heading home. Or you could make only two or three visits, allowing more time at each home. What is more important to us as pastors—quantity or quality? It seems to me that both pastor and parishioners benefit from unhurried visits—at least those visits which give the impression of being unhurried. Even one good visit a day is far better than three or four mediocre experiences that leave ministers worn out and church members frustrated.

Initiative, Invitation, and Spontaneity

A minister has one great advantage over most other helping professions. While others have to wait for people to approach them, the pastor has the freedom to go to persons when there is a need. It behooves us to take advantage of this initiative that is part of ministry.

Should we make an appointment for a visit or be spontaneous? In surveying a group of pastors on this question, I found the approach for visitation to homes divided about evenly. There are advantages and disadvantages to both. When an appointment is made beforehand, you are assured that the people will be at home. But such advance notice could start them worrying about the purpose of the visit or the appearance of the house. When making such an appointment it is helpful to set the minds of people at ease. Let them know why you are coming. Assure them that a lot of fussing is unnecessary if you sense this could be a problem.

When using the spontaneous approach, you have the immediate advantage of being there in person. Sometimes people might want to talk to the minister but anxiety prompts them to come up with an excuse when you try setting up a visit. With your appearance in person, such an anxiety barrier is sometimes diminished. A good visit can be the result. This is not to say that a minister should ever be "pushy" in home visitation. Tact, good common sense, and perceptiveness on the pastor's part are extremely important here. If the situation does not look conducive to a good visit, you can suggest setting up a more convenient time. Another advantage of spontaneous visiting is that it gives you a more flexible schedule. You are not bound to a particular day and time should a crisis situation arise. Some ministers prefer to have the hours, days, and weeks firmly scheduled. Others choose to be more open in their daily planning, to respond to circumstances as they develop, as well as to their own frame of mind. If you find yourself physically and emotionally drained, you can change your plans without disappointing people.

Problems in Scheduling Visits

Most of us live rather hectic lives in ministry. Therefore the question could well be raised: How can pastors today contact most church members in their homes? Evening meetings seem to be a necessary part of a minister's week, and parishioners, save the very elderly or parents with preschool children, are often gone during the day. So when does the pastor visit? And even when a visit is arranged, might not the members resent the pastor taking their time?

It is my conviction that ministers should visit people in their homes when there is both a need and an opportunity to do so. Certainly there are many commitments in the lives of both pastor and parishioners. Yet even during a busy week it is surprising how we can find time to do the things we believe important. As I worked on my professional project, nineteen persons were visited four times each over a two-month period. Looking back on this experience I am amazed that such a schedule could have been arranged and that those visited were able to see me. Most church members seem to welcome pastoral visits to their homes and make room for them. I also came to believe that most pastors can find the time when they realize the positive influence such visits can have. If most weeknights are filled, a Saturday or Sunday might provide some time when people are around the house. More family members may be at home on a weekend but this could work to our advantage as pastors. We can see firsthand the working relationship of the family and gain insight for ministry to them.

Number and Length of Visits

With the various pressures on pastors today, how many noncrisis home visits can we be expected to make even when their importance is recognized? Of the ministers contacted for my survey, the most frequent reason cited for not making more home visits was that too many other areas of ministry (preaching, administration, meetings, crisis visits, and counseling) took priority. I recall attending worship recently in a large congregation in the Northeast. A new pastor had just begun his ministry at this church. He led the worship service confidently and well. During the announcements, however, he mentioned several church members who were confined to their homes, unable to get out to worship. As he mentioned the names, it was evident that he felt badly that he had not yet been able personally to visit these people. Deep down I believe that most pastors want personal contact with their parishioners. Finding (or making!) the time is the issue.

Most of the pastors surveyed also indicated that they made an average of two to seven noncrisis home visits each week, with one hour as the approximate time for each visit. If an hour is usually allotted to a pastoral counseling session in the office, it seems that no less time should be set aside for a home visit if it is to be effective. There are ministers who rush around from home to hospital to home, staying no longer than to say hello and good-bye, one foot always apparently out the door. After a hurried prayer, they are off to the next place. Such visitation can soon wear out a minister and confuse the parishioners. This emphasis on quantity might produce impressive statistics but is ultimately demoralizing.

It is my feeling that a noncrisis home visit should seldom last less than nor much more than an hour. Two hours may seem justified in certain crisis visits. However, we can never really be sure what concerns will be raised during the time together. Sometimes serious concerns can be pursued in the pastor's office following initial attention during the home visit. I have often found that older adults especially seem reluctant to see the visit end. They like to have the minister stay beyond the hour length. This may partly be attributed to the loneliness many elderly people feel. Or it might reflect a past time when the pace of life and ministry were much slower and pastors could spend a whole afternoon with a particular family. It has been my experience that for this day and age an hour in a home seems in most cases to be a good length of time for a visit.

The Pastoral Conversation

The foundation for any effective pastoral conversation on a home visit is that both pastor and church member are relaxed. The familiar surrounding of the home should help the parishioner here. But what about the minister? How do we put ourselves at ease before making the visit? I find it helpful to think and pray briefly about the visit before making it. What are my attitudes toward these people? What is my reason for making this visit? Anxiety is lessened when I am clear in my own mind why I am going. I also try to review the records from any visits or other pastoral contacts previously made with these people. This helps to build constructively upon my pastoral work with parishioners, as well as determine some kind of direction for the time together. Of course this much preparation cannot and should not always be done. Sometimes spontaneity is the greatest attribute of home visits. At times the minister will find an initial questioning, spoken or unspoken, as to what the real motive is in being there. I found some people surprised and even relieved to discover that my main reason in visiting was to provide the opportunity for coming to know one another better. So many persons are conditioned to having others approach them as a means of getting something. To have someone visit simply because one is interested in the people is refreshing.

If these persons have not been visited previously, conversation can be initiated by raising questions about family members or making positive comments on features of the home. If sincere, such comments are usually welcome. In some cases I jot down a few questions beforehand to help start the conversation. While periods of silence are not always bad in pastoral conversation, I have found that it is usually better for the time together to have movement. Yet a feeling of rush should be avoided. People need to have the opportunity to share some of their deeper concerns if they wish.

During the home visit we want to assure people that we are not there to judge, discover hidden family secrets, or recruit them for another church job. Rather, we are there as pastors because we care about them and somehow want to convey that caring through our behavior and words. Listening is certainly an important part of such caring—listening for questions and messages that may not always be expressed in words. Why is she sitting so rigidly with her arms folded like that? Why does he always seem to try to speak for her? Why does he remind me of a volcano about to erupt? Is there an anger about life? The church? Themselves? What emotions do such attitudes touch off in me as a minister and person? How do we deal with these feelings in our parishioners? This brings us to our next question.

Pastoral Counseling on a Home Visit?

There is a scene that is familiar to many pastors. You are visiting a parishioner in his or her home or apartment. As the conversation develops, the member sighs and says, "Pastor, there is something I need to talk to somebody about." What follows is the sharing of a problem that needs immediate attention. What should the minister do? Some of us have been trained that under no circumstances should pastoral counseling be conducted in homes. An appointment should immediately be set up in the study. Yet this rigidly professional approach has some disadvantages. We can underestimate the trust and courage necessary for a parishioner to confide a personal concern. When such a problem is shared it seems that, as ministers, we need somehow to address it immediately. Many people do not easily approach us to make an appointment in our study. The familiarity of the home might well enable a person to feel at ease enough to make known a concern. To avoid at least initial discussion of the problem could convey a negative message about caring on our part. If the concern is of a long-standing nature that will not be resolved quickly, our office would be the best place to continue. But the responses to this question of the twenty-four ministers surveyed are revealing. Fifteen said they often engaged in pastoral counseling on a home visit when there was a need. Five stated that they sometimes did. The majority felt the need for immediacy in dealing with a parishioner's problem rather than risk the wait for a more formal setting in their study. Next week or even tomorrow might prove to be too late.

What personal concerns are most often brought up by parishioners during home visits? Pastors listed the following: marital and family problems, conflict with other church members, depression, drug or alcohol abuse, poor health, lack of affirmation, loneliness, finances, faith, occupation, world situation, legal matters, school, relatives, and relationships with others. It seemed evident from the survey that many pastors see home visitation as an important instrument of pastoral care.

Concluding the Conversation

Bringing the home visit to an end is an art that needs to be handled tactfully. When you feel the conversation has proceeded long enough, you might say something such as: "I am glad for this opportunity to have visited with you. Thank you for the coffee," and so forth (if there were refreshments). Standing up is a more final way of showing the visit is over, but again this needs to be done with tact. At times such words or actions may prompt a parishioner to share what is really on his or her mind. The pastor has to judge at this point whether it would be better to stay longer or to set another appointment.

Some people will consistently be disappointed when you give indication to leave. Most will realize that others also need your attention. It is important not to overstay a welcome. If there suddenly seems to be more activity around the house which evidently needs the attention of those being visited, or if the parishioners are giving off impatient signals such as looking at a watch, this might indicate a conversation should end. But the pastor should never be the one to give off busy signals during a visit. We are there to be available—to listen and minister as we are able. How the parishioners respond is their choice. My experience is that most will respond well and return the caring.

But there are some parishioners who cannot or will not respond positively to our visitation. Such visits may be characterized with strained conversation and many silences. As ministers, we are called at times to deal with the hostility of and rejection from others. This is never easy to do, but we seek to follow Christ, who set the good example.

Social Visits to Homes

There are times when the pastor is invited to the home of a parishioner for a social occasion either alone with wife or husband, or with the entire family, as the case may be. Should such an event be considered a pastoral visit? I am inclined to say yes. Parishioners do not invite the pastor to their home, regardless of how informal the circumstance, because they have nothing better to do or no one else to ask. In the midst of light conversation parishioners may be trying to ask questions about their family or faith. Certainly part of the reason for inviting you is to know you better as a person. But you are still the pastor to them, someone special in their thinking—more special than you may realize. We need to be aware of the importance of such social gatherings in homes. While the purpose is one of relaxation, we should not forget some of the deeper opportunities offered by such invitations.

Keeping a Record

Should records of pastoral visits be kept? On the attitudinal survey one minister wrote "no" and likened this practice to the pharisees' approach. I find such an opinion difficult to understand. Are other professions—physicians, lawyers, psychologists, social workers—also to be condemned for keeping notes and records on the people with whom they work? Certainly our work with parishioners is no less important. Nor is our power of recall any greater than that of these members of other helping professions. The survey mentioned indicated that approximately half the pastors kept some sort of record on visits, while others for various reasons did not. I can state only how keeping records on pastoral visits has helped my ministry.

The method I use is simple. In a notebook I list the names of all church members. Following each name are twelve squares for the months. I have various symbols for different kinds of pastoral visits—hospital, membership (home), crisis (home) and noncrisis (home). Following each visit I note the type of call made. This simple record helps my ministry in several ways. It enables me to see at a glance how many visits are being made at a particular time as well as the kinds of visits. It also lets me see the pattern and frequency of visits to various parishioners. This information can be useful as I evaluate my pastoral care in the congregation. When the annual church business meeting is held I can, if I choose, be more specific about my ministry during the past year.

In another notebook I keep a record of my impressions from a pastoral visit. At the top of the page I place the name of the person. Following the date of the visit I write a brief summary of the conversation. I try to recall significant comments and set down my observations of the visit. Such a record enables me to build upon previous visits. Few of us have photographic memories. With the passing of time, details can be lost to our thinking. Records help us to recall important comments and recurring concerns in the lives of our parishioners. Certain details from previous conversations such as names of extended family members or the correct names of illnesses can be jotted down in the notebook. When the next visit is made, we have these details in mind and this contributes to the impression that we care.

Help to Preaching

A brief comment should be made on how a home visit might help with preaching. This is one of the "pluses" with home visits. Visits help us understand some of the particular concerns and pressures our people are facing. These concerns could then contribute toward our sermons as we try to address the needs of persons with the gospel. But ministers should be very cautious in using situations from home visits as illustrations in preaching, even when no names are used. This is especially true with visits made in the current pastorate. Such use of pastoral material would go far in destroying trust.

Dealing with Sexual Attraction

There is another aspect of home visits that can discourage pastors from trying them more often. How do we handle our feelings of sexual attraction? Some pastors avoid this very real question by never making a visit where such is a possibility. Other ministers have their wives or husbands accompany them. Yet in having spouses accompany the pastor, effective pastoral care could be blocked. Concerns that need to be discussed may never be mentioned.

Certainly there have been enough "humorous" stories circulated in seminaries, ministers' meetings, and church gatherings concerning embarrassing circumstances or questionable motives in pastoral visitation. Such remarks only reflect the uncertainty and confusion regarding this area of ministry. The time has come to reclaim a mature attitude toward home visits such as we see in the ministries of such spiritual giants as Martin Luther, Richard Baxter, John Wesley, Washington Gladden, and other more recent leaders in pastoral care.

As pastors we need to be in touch with our motives and feelings for any facet of ministry, including home visitation. We need to know why we are making a particular visit. If we find ourselves going more because of our own unmet needs rather than to help others in the love of Christ, there will always be a danger. Discretion must be shown when making home visits. If we feel uneasy about the circumstances of such a meeting, we can ask if it could be rescheduled for the office. If this is not possible, it may be helpful to make such a visit when other family members such as children are also home. It is important that ministers as well as parishioners feel comfortable about the circumstances of the visit. Pastors can usually take the initiative in setting the circumstances in which the personal call will be made.

The result of any home visit depends upon the motives and attitudes that individual ministers bring to it. More than any other profession today, the pastorate offers a day or night accessibility to other people. This is a sacred trust. Any pastor with integrity will keep this trust firmly in mind as home visits are made. Although there is no simple rule that would cover all situations for home visitation, I find wisdom and comfort from the words of Scripture:

> Do not rebuke an older man, but exhort him as you would a father; treat younger men like brothers, older women like mothers, younger women like sisters, in all purity (I Timothy 5:1-2).

6

Training Lay Persons for Visitation

Why should church people be trained for home visits? As important as home visits are, hospital and crisis home visits take precedence in pastoral ministry. But lay people can be trained to make friendly visits to the homes of other church members, bringing the skill of listening and the gift of concern. This kind of lay ministry frees the pastor to visit where the need is greatest.

Lay people should also be trained to make home visits because of our conviction about the ministry of all believers. God showers gifts on all Christians and expects us to use them responsively. Some parishioners have the gifts of kindness, interest in others, perceptiveness, and tact which are needed to be an effective visitor. We need to give opportunity for church members to develop and use such gifts.

Distinctions of a Pastoral Visit

There is, however, a distinction between the pastoral and lay visit that needs to be stated. There is something unique about a pastor visiting parishioners which a lay person cannot completely emulate. One of the great Protestant preachers of the present day recently stated that theological trends during the past twenty years have not always, as hoped, turned lay people into ministers. Too often conviction of the "ministry of all believers" has been misinterpreted; the minister has become more like the lay person. How does this insight relate to visitation in the church today? I see three interrelated dimensions that make pastoral visitation unique.

First, most ordained pastors today have spent the equivalent of three full years taking courses in applied ministry. Many ministers have kept up their training with continuing education. An increasing number are pursuing advanced degrees in the area of church studies. Such training brings a particular depth to pastoral visitation that is not possible for most lay visitors.

Second, the minister usually has an acquaintance with each person in the congregation as well as a grasp of the church's overall operation which other church members seldom have. A good pastor will make a home visit knowing the background of the parishioners, being aware of how the church functions, and having a good idea of where these people should be fitting into the Body. Who else in the church could lay claim to this kind of perspective?

These two points of distinction give rise to the third unique characteristic of the pastoral visit: the ability to counsel parishioners when there is need. Pastors, because of their training and knowledge of a congregation, are in a position to offer counseling when circumstances permit. Most lay people are unequipped to deal directly with family or personal problems when they are brought up during a visit, but they can develop a sensitivity to tensions in a family that may need to be faced. The pastor needs to be in communication with lay visitors regarding the results of their calling in order that follow-up can take place when necessary.

The above three qualities distinguishing pastoral from lay visits may be summarized by the word "professional." An ordained pastor with an earned degree in the study of the church and ministry should be a professional. Such a person is expected to have the skills and knowledge in the practice of ministry that sets her or him apart from most other church members. Yet the difference is one of function rather than importance, for all members of the church body—the body of Christ—are essential

(1 Corinthians 12:14-26). Certainly the gifts of kindness, good listening, and the love of Christ are as much in evidence among lay persons as among pastors. These gifts need to be developed and used within and beyond the congregation. Pastors cannot be everywhere at once. Lay people making friendly visits on others can both supplement and complement the work of the professional minister in a very positive way.

A Friendly Visitors Team

There is a group in our congregation called the Friendly Visitors. We meet bimonthly on a weekday night for a two-hour meeting in different homes. The group consists of eight people. Acting as coordinator and resource for these parishioners, I help them make visits on other church members.

We begin with conversation and prayer, followed by reports on any visits made since the previous meeting. If pastoral follow-up seems needed on any person visited, I note it. New assignments are discussed for each team member. I also try to share some of my own learning and experience in visitation.

When the group began, a list of guidelines for making home visits was developed. This list came partially from my own experience in making home visits, but also contained insights from these lay people. Suggestions on good listening provide another important resource for us. Copies of these resources will be found at the close of the chapter. We are presently using Willard Callender's book *How to Make a Friendly Call* (Valley Forge: Judson Press, 1982) as a basis for planning visitation. Our scope has expanded to include visits to hospitals and nursing homes, but the primary emphasis is still upon home visitation.

Our visitors group developed from my professional project mentioned in chapter 2. Before making home visits for my own research, I invited some persons in the congregation to meet with me as a support group. I shared with them the purpose of the project, the reasons for home visits in ministry, and other relevant materials in this area of pastoral care. We even role-played a pastoral visit to the home.

Following completion of my visits for the project, I invited this group, along with those I had been visiting, to meet with me and help evaluate the work. During this time together I suggested the idea of beginning a team of lay visitors in our church and invited those present to participate. Questions were raised by these people, such as "do people want just the pastor to visit?" and "how do we assure those being visited that we just want to get to know each other better?" This last question is, of course, frequently faced in home visits whether we are pastors or lay people.

This is how our Friendly Visitors team developed. Such a group could begin in many ways and in various church settings. Individuals could be contacted in person, by phone, or invited by letter. Such a group should probably not be open to just anyone from the congregation who wants to volunteer. Persons with certain qualities are needed—compassion, good listening ability, tact, perceptiveness, and being a good team player. These qualities can be developed to an extent, but there should be evidence of some or all these gifts in people before they are invited to join the group.

Is this being exclusive in the church body? The emphasis here needs to be on different functions rather than on the personal worth of each church member. The apostle Paul talks about the various personal gifts in 1 Corinthians 12. When we look at the ministry of Jesus and how he gathered his disciples, what do we see? He did not make an announcement asking for volunteers. Rather, Jesus personally chose twelve very different persons. There is an important lesson in his approach for us in ministry today. Church members with strong needs for recognition and influence will be hindered in their effectiveness as visitors. They could also disrupt the development of the group's life. People who do not evidence the qualities for good visitation should gently be encouraged to serve the church in another capacity. Sometimes, however, such selectivity is not a real option for the pastor. This is especially true in a smaller congregation where the range of available and willing volunteers is limited. We have to do the best we can in developing such a visitation team with care, integrity and—last but not least—patience.

Guidelines for Friendly Visitation

1. Before visiting, learn all you can about the persons to be visited. What is their life situation? Still working or retired?

Children? Married or single? Are they active in church? In what areas have they served?
2. Prepare some questions beforehand to help conversation. But don't feel that talk has to be nonstop! Periods of silence can sometimes be helpful, too.
3. Comments about interesting objects (pictures and so forth) in the home are a good way to start conversation.
4. If you stop by a home without having made an appointment, be ready to set another time if the circumstances are not convenient.
5. If you are visiting more than one person (a couple or a family), try to include everyone in the conversation.
6. Try walking in the other's shoes—what is life like for him or her?
7. If you feel too tired, don't make a visit. You won't be doing yourselves or the other person(s) a favor.
8. Before each visit, go over the "Listening Skills" suggestions, on page 60.
9. By what you say and do, you can assure people that you want to get to know them better, rather than get them to do something.
10. A visit should usually last no more than an hour; don't wear out your welcome. You will have to determine how long a stay is helpful.
11. Remember that through a visit, you will often receive more than you give.
12. Never argue, interrupt, or pass judgment too quickly.
13. Don't be overly discouraged if the visit doesn't go as well as you would have liked. Remember that your willingness to go to visit with a person means a lot in itself.
14. Let the person(s) being visited bring up questions about faith, rather than yourself.
15. At the close of the conversation, ask the person(s) if they would like to have a prayer. If so, offer a prayer, thanking God for this time together and asking that God's care and blessing continue in the lives of those visited.
16. Let the pastor know how the visit went and whether you feel follow-up would be helpful.

Listening Skills[1]

1. Show interest in and be understanding of the other person.
2. Show empathy when you sense it is needed.
3. If a problem is raised, try to listen for causes and help the other to see what might be done to improve the situation.
4. Learn how to be silent when silence is needed.
5. Listen prayerfully. We cannot listen to others until we have first listened to God.
6. Listen lovingly. When we listen to another, we should not try to label him or her as this or that "type." Respond to the person's soul, spirit, essence, dignity. Those who love, listen; and those who listen, love.
7. Listen humbly. In listening, there is no room for spiritual arrogance or pride. When we listen to the concerns of others, let us remember that we are not above the same kinds of potential problems.
8. Listen permissively. Let others be themselves.
9. Listen totally. Be sensitive to what is not said; observe body language.
10. Listen expectantly. Can we listen and convey to others that this is not the end, but a new beginning?

7

Conclusion

A great writer once remarked that the hardest thing about writing a book is the first word. But it seems to me that the last word is the real challenge. We have discussed the many dimensions of home visitation—the how, what, and when of such ministry. Going to persons where they live has been presented as an opportunity that few other professions have chosen to maintain. It would seem sad to me if the the pastoral ministry also abandoned the practice of home visits. Yet there are indications that the strategic importance of the home visit is being reclaimed by many ministers. The art of such visitation has deep roots in the history of God's people, as we have seen.

There is a phrase familiar to any parish minister: "Pastor, I know you must be busy. . . ." And so we are. Yet as we consider those who were the greatest help and influence in our own lives, who were they? Were they certain people who, though carrying heavy responsibilities and full schedules, somehow found the time to talk with us? There are many in the churches today who need to hear the same spoken and unspoken message from their pastor: "Yes, I'm busy, but I have time for you." The home visit offers an excellent opportunity to give this message to people.

I close with the words of William Croswell Doane who, in his poem "The Preacher's Mistake," expressed in a profound way the importance of pastoral contact with parishioners:

THE PARISH PRIEST
Of austerity,
Climbed up in a high church steeple
To be nearer God,
So that he might hand
His word down to His people.

When the sun was high,
When the sun was low,
The good man sat unheeding
Sublunary things.
From transcendency
Was he forever reading.

And now and again
When he heard the creak
Of the weather vane a-turning,
He closed his eyes
And said, "Of a truth
From God I now am learning."

And in sermon script
He daily wrote
What he thought was sent from heaven,
And he dropped this down
On his people's heads
Two times one day in seven.

In his age God said,
"Come down and die!"
And he cried out from the steeple,
"Where art thou, Lord?"
And the Lord replied,
"Down here among my people."[1]

May God give us the wisdom and grace to be among our people through pastoral visitation.

Notes

Chapter 2
[1] John T. McNeill, *A History of the Cure of Souls* (New York: Harper and Brothers, Publishers, Inc., 1951), p. 127.
[2] *Adventures in English Literature* (New York: Harcourt Brace Jovanovich, Inc., 1979), p. 54.
[3] Martin Luther, *Church and Ministry*, Part 2, in *Luther's Works*, edited by Conrad Bergendoff and Helmut T. Lehman, volume XL (Philadelphia: Fortress Press, 1958), p. 270.
[4] Nehemiah Curnock, ed., *The Journal of John Wesley* (New York: G. P. Putnam's Sons, 1963) pp. 113-114.
[5] Seward Hiltner, *Preface to Pastoral Theology* (Nashville: Abingdon Press, 1958), p. 83.
[6] Washington Gladden, *Church and Parish Problems* (New York: The Thwing Company, 1911), p. 184.
[7] Wayne E. Oates, *New Dimensions in Pastoral Care* (Philadelphia: Fortress Press, 1970), pp. 15-16.
[8] Paul Pruyser, *The Minister as Diagnostician: Personal Problems in Pastoral Perspective* (Philadelphia: The Westminster Press, 1976), p. 25.

Chapter 3
[1] Leonard Mosley, *Dulles* (New York: The Dial Press, 1978), pp. 47-48.
[2] Taylor Caldwell, *The Listener* (New York: Doubleday & Co., Inc., 1960), pp. 4-5, 15-16.

Chapter 4
[1] For this section on pastoral visitation to mental hospitals I am indebted to the insights of the Rev. Robert Baker, an Episcopal priest and supervisor of

pastoral services at the Marlboro State Hospital, Monmouth County, New Jersey.
[2] Lawrence Baulch, *Return to the World* (Valley Forge: Judson Press, 1968), pp. 95, 190-191.
[3] Marie Buckley, *Breaking into Prison* (Boston: Beacon Press, 1974), p. 15.

Chapter 5
[1] W. McFerrin Stowe, *If I Were a Pastor* (Nashville: Abingdon Press, 1983), p. 31.

Chapter 6
[1] Adapted from Harry Farra, "Your Ministry of Listening," *Baptist Leader*, October, 1980, pp. 45-46.

Chapter 7
[1] Hazel Felleman, ed., *The Best Loved Poems of the American People* (Garden City, N.Y.: Garden City Books, 1936). pp. 339-340.